Weather Watchers

Wind

Cassie Mayer

Heinemann Library
Chicago, Illinois

Photo research by Tracy Cummins, Tracey Engel, and Ruth Blair
Designed by Jo Hinton-Malivoire
Printed by Hi-Liter Graphics

10 09 08
10 9 8 7 6 5 4 3 2

Library of Congress Cataloging-in-Publication Data
Mayer, Cassie.
  Wind / Cassie Mayer.-- 1st ed.
      p. cm. -- (Weather watchers)
  Includes bibliographical references and index.
  ISBN-13: 978-1-4034-8412-3 (library binding-hardcover : alk. paper)
  ISBN-10: 1-4034-8412-0 (library binding-hardcover : alk. paper)
  ISBN-13: 978-1-4034-8420-8 (pbk. : alk. paper)
  ISBN-10: 1-4034-8420-1 (pbk. : alk. paper)
  1. Winds--Juvenile literature. 2. Weather--Juvenile literature. I. Title. II. Series.
  QC931.4.M39 2007
  551.51'8--dc22
                                          2006007908

Acknowledgments
The author and publisher are grateful to the following for permission to reproduce copyright material:
Alamy p. **15** (Michael Dwyer); Corbis pp. **4** (cloud; rain, Anthony Redpath), **5** (C/B Productions), **7** (George H. H. Huey). **9**, **11** (Lowell Georgia), **13** (China Newsphoto/Reuters), **14** (Lawrence Manning), **19** (Jim Reed/Jim Reed Photography), **20** (epa/Anatoly Maltsev), **21** (Ariel Skelley), **23** (hurricane, Jim Reed/Jim Reed Photography); Getty pp. **4** (lightning; snow, Marc Wilson Photography), **6** (Bob Elsdale), **8** (The Image Bank/Laurence Dutton), **10** (Panoramic Images), **12** (Asia Images/Mary Grace Long), **16** (National Geographic/Gordon Wiltsie), **18** (A T Willet), **23** (tornado, A T Willet); Shutterstock p. **22** (windsock with wind, Steven Robertson; windsock with no wind, Anders Brownworth; weather vane, Robert Kyllo; windmill, Barry Hurt).

Cover photograph reproduced with permission of Corbis (Royalty Free).
Back cover photgraph reproduced with permission of China Newsphoto/Reuters.

Every effort has been made to contact copyright holders of any material reproduced in this book. Any omissions will be rectified in subsequent printings if notice is given to the publisher.

Contents

What Is Weather?

Weather is what the air is like outside. Weather can change all the time.

A windy day is a type of weather.

What Is Wind?

Wind is moving air.

Wind moves in many directions.

You can feel wind.

You can see wind move things around.

Wind moves across land.

Wind moves across water.

Wind can be gentle.

Wind can be strong.

What Does Wind Do?

Wind moves air around the world.
Wind can bring warm air.

14

Wind can bring cold air.

Types of Wind

Some winds change direction every day.
Mountain winds can change direction
every day.

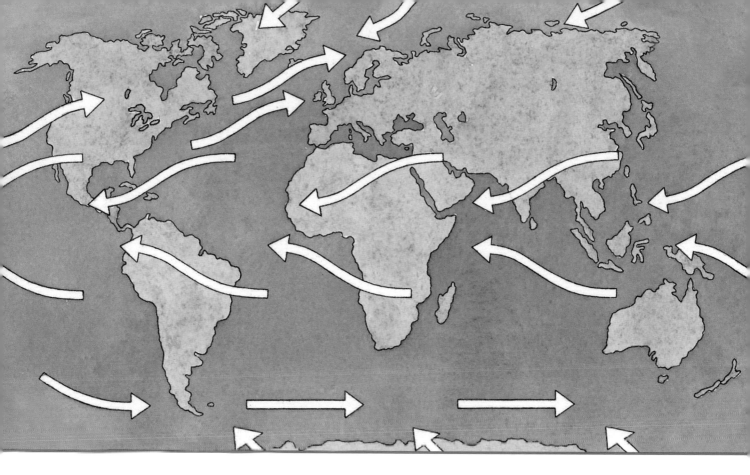

Some winds blow the same direction
for a while. Ocean winds can stay the
same direction for a while.

17

Dangerous Winds

A tornado is made of spinning air. It has very strong winds.

A hurricane is a strong storm.
It has very strong winds.

How Does Wind Help Us?

Wind can bring rain.
Wind can bring a sunny day.

Wind is an important part of our
weather. Wind can also be fun!

Wind Tools

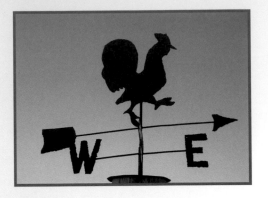

This is a weather vane. It shows which direction the wind is blowing.

These are windmills. They use the wind to make things work.

This is a wind sock. It shows which direction the wind is blowing. It also shows how hard the wind is blowing.

Picture Glossary

 **hurricane** a big storm with strong winds

 **tornado** a tower of air that spins very fast

Index

Note to Parents and Teachers

This series introduces children to the concept of weather and its importance in our lives. Discuss with children the types of weather that they are already familiar with, and point out how weather changes season by season.

In this book, children explore wind. The photographs were selected to engage children while supporting the concepts presented in the book. The text has been chosen with the advice of a literacy expert to enable beginning readers success reading independently or with moderate support. An expert in the field of meteorology was consulted to ensure accurate content. You can support children's nonfiction literacy skills by helping them use the table of contents, headings, picture glossary, and index.